INTERSECTIONS

ACKNOWLEDGEMENT

'My Gramma Cleo' first appeared in *The Balm of Dusk Lilies*, The Observer Literary Series, 2001.

INTERSECTIONS

A COLLECTION OF POEMS

FRANCES-MARIE COKE

Poetry series editor: Kwame Dawes

PEEPAL TREE

First published in Great Britain in 2010
Peepal Tree Press Ltd
17 King's Avenue
Leeds LS6 1QS
UK

ISBN 13: 9781845230883

Supported by
**ARTS COUNCIL
ENGLAND**

CONTENTS

PART ONE

... Of Soldier Crabs and River Women and
a Mother Stitching...

PARTING AT IDLEWILD

I begin here but there were other beginnings –
the taut, dusky valleys of Above Rocks,
tenement sides where landlords railed
against barefooted broods, and tenants gulped
their share of twice-breathed air, balancing the rent,
sighing out their lives, worrying at the feet
they miscounted for new shoes.

The lustre bleeding from pubescent love,
my mother tied her belly, washed me in the stream
of her regret, bundled me in my father's arms
and we were bound for another place. There,
I watched the disappearing rainbow of her skirt
until it was a speck of green, then nothing –
me without their shoulders, in that flaming sun,
that salt that stung the water from my eyes.

Idlewild: I couldn't say your name
but I would be your child – curled like a comma
in your sentence, sheltered in your grey and indigo;
you my anchor in the storm, my promise of first light;
my face framed in a woolly thicket, straining yellow ribbons,
or on my belly with my dress spread out
across the floor, bare feet in the air, fingers tensed
above another page in this new book
transporting me from my disconnected island,

from that bleak place behind the Junction Road,

from that house where lizards lined
loose skirting-boards and slithered down grey walls;
where broken windows swung
half-naked on their rusty hinges, with burnt-out
chiffon curtains gathered at each end,
elastic fraying at the edges
of that town without the sea, without a song.

IDLEWILD NIGHTS

Down from the fretwork of the dining hall,
past the breakfront, where December crockery
rested through the year, past Dadda's piano,
keys yellowing with the seasons,
keeping time with swirls and scrawls faded
from the tattered pages he uncurled
across a frame, tracing clefs and trebles,
as his home-schooled fingers raised the songs
that changed Galina's hat shop to a church,
a children's stage, a lover's breath, a dream.

Out on the veranda wrapped round the house,
where croakers changed their slimy skins
and slithered down the peeling grey to slip
our busy eyes, Gramma rocked the wicker chair,
sweeping back my hair,
spinning tales, easing in the night
with Mary and the Baby, Anancy and
Tookomah, Charge of the Light Brigade
and hosts of golden daffodils she'd never seen
but knew by heart. She murmured stilling melodies
of all things bright and beautiful, (sowing seeds
for dreams of copper pennies wedged between
my jam jars of paradise plum and mint-balls)
and yes, Jesus loves me, the bible tells me so.
Nestling me against her breast, she closed,
the door on all the shifting worlds I'd left behind.

ABOVE ROCKS

Left turn from the crossroads at the top of Stony Hill,
Mr. Excel's red-seam bus belched and chugged,
groaning up Parks Road draped
in razor grass and whistling bamboo that hugged
the glistening edge of a dismal river,
snaked up to the piazza at the village shop
to let us off across the street
from tilting houses whose windows slanted
on worn-out hinges; and we dragged out old newspaper
stuffed inside our blouses to keep away bad feeling.

This was no Idlewild: too many lurking trails,
no infinite sapphire dome above the sea
to urge imagination past the sullen cocoa leaves
that gossiped day and night; not a book in sight!

This mishmash of yabba yards leaning out for light
was home to Grannie Gillies, a woman without colour –
her skin stretched on prickled blood, raisin freckles bunched
in stubborn patterns – her hair, dry as coconut husks,
framing a crimson rage that lined her lips
and set her eyes ablaze, soured by the bitter brew
she sipped from life and chipped enamel mugs,
and dry mouthfuls of regret and shame she gulped
with her Quaker Oats from a cardboard box.

Day broke in Above Rocks on a dozen feet
trekking half-asleep down to the river in a clatter
of long-mouth goblets, rusting pans, dented basins,
pots that spent too many days on fire.
We trudged through grass that sawed our shins,
drawing blood we couldn't see till daylight.

Behind the gutted heels of impatient feet,
children drew back, 'fraid for River Mumma and
her duppies guarding the Golden Table,
until the parting of the mist
undressed the river in its shining silence, dispersing
rumours of strange spirits harboured by the night.

MOONLIGHT CIRCLES

None of these beginnings was mine
like Idlewild – her soft black earth slipping through
our fingers as we rummaged through the cellar,
scouting out half-inch holes for wrigglers scrambling
round our feet to our chant of "nanny, nanny",
calling insects, shrieking when the ants replied –
their armies lugging beads of guava jam and crackers
that drew them to the trail of forty legs.

Evening brought the softening light
of peenie-wallie bottles, brown girl in de ring,
moonlight circles in the grass where we shuffled,
roasted peanuts to "Finga mash, no cry",
and missing that refrain, burying our wounds,
we wept between the folds of Gramma's skirt, sighing
for the cadences of her "never mind".

Idlewild my comfort! How you emptied
round the corner to Galina, through the burial ground
at Wilderness where we scampered from the ten-foot
blackheart man and rollin' calf rattling at our heels –
big 'fraid trembling up ahead with little 'fraid in tow.

Galina: where the morning sun just glanced
and seaside palms stretched out dry
in rainbow ribbons, waiting for church women
to come sashaying in on sunbeams, sporting
floral and bandana tie-heads, and puss boots
lately from the market at Port Maria Bay.

They came to spin their straw,
weaving weft and warp, stringing hairpin rugs,
sewing eyes on black rag-dolls black children didn't want.

They came up from the alley where no-one spoke
in future tense, dizzy yearnings gathering momentum
in their bellies: Galina women
teasing life from severed threads of empire.

TWO WOMEN OF IDLEWILD

It seemed they only smiled at secrets
in the kitchen – and even then
it wasn't always clear if you watched
their mouths – it was the wrinkles in the corners

of their eyes – at the crackling fireside,
with roas' breadfruit and rundown steaming
on the table, laid out with slivered pear and fry
plantain; or over patchwork bedspreads

winking in the sun. Then Gramma and
Louise were on one side, their differences
smoothed out, like starched blue shirts
and crochet runners ironed stiff

with spitting metal from the hissing coals.
On Saturdays they scrubbed the bloody wooden
floor with Seville-orange, buffing it with brushes
old men carved from dry coconuts,

as rowdy uncles stalked the bubbling pumpkin
soup, with fresh beef bone from Little Bay
and scattered thyme leaves floating on
the riches of the Dutchie; cornmeal

pudden simmering in coc'nut cream,
a dozen cousins fanned flames to chants of
"Hell atop, hell a bottom,
hallelujah in the middle!"

Divided by the doors into the house,
different shades of brown-skin gal minding
a dozen babies between them,
Miss Phillips and her servant ached

the same dry ache for missing men
at labour in the fields, feeding the scattered empire,
wept the same hot tears in home-stitched 'kerchiefs –
two women with one longing in their eyes.

WOMEN OF THE STRAW

They came in threes to Idlewild:
each woman with her basket and a child
at play behind her homespun skirt. They came
with needle marks and swollen fingers,

eyes fixed on their toes, their wistful sighs
for morning sun to dry the sallow straw
so they could twist and sew it,
stitching out their days in perfect circles.

              The rainbow gone,
they edged away in silence, shuffling coins
and counting infants, fearing the lust of men
who whispered promises in the leaves,
but brought them savage night instead –
their panting snuffing dreams that flickered
in the kerosene light – leaving
the drizzle in their eyes to mourn
the hidden injuries of love's sweet thorn.

THE MAKING OF A STRAW HAT

The frond must first be dried and then
they stretch it, deftly plaiting in and out
until a snake worth sixty cents a yard
surrounds their feet, enisling them along

the edges of their wretched speck of earth
skirted by the sea. Now lost among the sheaves,
now visible, their fingers work the straw,
threads and needles straight, battling frayed edges.

Long wooden benches stretch from end to end
of drawn-out days. Above their sweating hands,
their faces motionless and vague, they sigh
at children's feet outgrowing brand new shoes.

Sometimes their eyes turn to the corner;
the voices fade; they whisper of another fallen
half-grown girl some man gave a belly
before she learned to plait or turn or sew.

Their nightmares are of stepping off this island
into eternity, knowing nothing but dry straw;
of reeking kerosene lamps with burnt-out wicks.
Their nightmares are of circles drawn too tight

shrinking into shapeless hats nobody wants.

KINGSTON STREETS

From the pages where I roamed in Idlewild,
at one with everything in Little Bay, Galina

and the winding trails to Goldeneye,
I landed in a world where no one plaited straw,

where beds wore home-stitched sheets and
pale chenille bedspreads, never patchwork quilts.

Streets in Kingston, where we lived, narrowed
into lanes – most of them dead-ends.

Day and night my mother stitched the pounds
of cloth she stretched beyond her purse

to dress us, switching gatherer and bobbin,
easing tension, steadying the selvages

of slippery days, swerving in and out
of corners, treading water with the presser foot,

fighting life with thread and needle,
sidestepping shears and fortune's wheel.

At her feet I heaped up memory gems and warnings,
with scraps for sleeves and collars, clothes for dolls

with broken necks. When nothing from the pickings matched,
she trimmed with bias binding – every spoil a style!

And when her face grew weary of my unanswerable
questions, I slinked away with the Bobsey Twins,

pressed my back against the almond tree
beside the fence, building castles from loose stones.

Fingering their polished smoothness side by side
with their bruising edges, my childish musing

turned on contradictions, like her two-faced
reassurances I always doubted ("every disappointment

is for good and those who leave do love you").
And so it was in later years, in scattered places,

these scraps would come back uninvited –
haunting me in nightmares where I walked half-naked;

wearing what my mother couldn't finish –
spaces in long passages of callow, mottled times.

SOMETIMES, MY MOTHER...

Sometimes my mother's sweat bathed us —
soft morning dewdrops washing hurt away,
beading on our blossoms, slaking thirsty leaves.
Her smile, fresh sunrise, turned
back night's pain. When she fought
a lightning storm raged — noon-heat
bearing down on life's mean streak;
madness thrashing out at losses undeserved.

At times my mother's tears drowned
her courage; rivulets of sorrow, tell-tale
sighs she couldn't hide. At other times
her eyes were gentle evening sunset
coming to terms with approaching dusk,
swallowing swords and scissors;
resigning herself to herself, holding still
to her needle, circling the patterns of time.

REPLACING ROSES

His skin was always cold and pale
against the inky night. He slinked
into the sheets to dull the fragrance
of a budding rose, besmirching it
with rancid sweat, his sickening fingers
tracing all about her as she shrank
into the darkness, her knuckles edged
against the margin of a bed
that shuddered with his weight.

By day she scampered to hidden corners,
pressed herself into the shady corridors;
the startled eyes of others fixed upon
her strangeness – this child who curled her lips
and sulked into the fading paint splashed against
the silence of a house that wasn't home.
No-one asked. She never said.

Outside, against the picket fence, they snatched
the cankered rose bush from the ground,
planting gerberas instead;
they watered fresh new blossoms
stretching out their slivered petals.
Everyone agreed; these were hardier than
the roses. She gathered up her stillborn buds,
pressed them in the pages of her book
and turned the switch inside her heart to off.

RIVER WOMEN

Behind their barely-covered lips,
The Whisperers of Above Rocks huddled
in the no man's land where housetops leaned

and clotheslines tilted, their arms akimbo
jutting out from hilly backsides, fingers jabbing
at each other's brows, presiding over business

in the valley. Wielding bramble brooms
dragged across their piece of dust,
they swept up kass-kass with cut-eye,

frock-tail fanning an' kiss-teet, passing sentence
on grudgefulness and bad mind, malice and red-eye –
hot words spiced with vinegar and scotch bonnet.

They planted after-births and futures at the navel-string tree;
washed away bad luck with sinklebible and baptized
in healing streams; read meanings in the wind,

in deadening stares of three-foot horse, dogs
howling at full moons, headless sen-seh fowls fluttering
in the feathered blood spilled in time for Sunday lunch.

Long-robed, heads wrapped in calico, they journeyed
down dark mud-tracks to their sideways church,
there to sip white rum and rule the nine-night sankey.

Their faces wore each other's rage and everything
that caused it – (one more half-empty butterpan
de pickney bring up wid him two lef-han from riverside!).

They railed at daughters sent to better life in town,
ending up in bed and *in the way* for men
with nothing but their curly hair and two-toned shoes.

No yard was spared from throw-word
when river women draped their wash-pans with their legs,
flared their noses and their skirts, (tucked in where it mattered),

and punished the missis white sheets with Guinea Gold
and corn cob, muttering underneath their breaths
when stains betrayed dark secrets of Old Stony Hill.

By sunset they'd passed judgement on everything
that counted: clear skin, dark skin, brown skin –
each with its own grade, depending on the hair –

knotty-knotty, picky-picky, good or nice and long –
every version praised or damned at the river-bank,
every son instructed how to lighten with a nice brown girl.

In time we knew our verdict: "Miss G. gran-pickney dem
have good colour and nice hair, but dat one wid
de mawga foot, she want some good home-training!"

The river murmured, minding its own business.

THE RAGE OF GRANNIE GILLIES

Wrung out among the stories from the river,
the simmered rage of Grannie Gillies found itself
dissected and concluded: "Not a soul inside
de yard do har anything! She and her half-coolie
husband come up here from Portland. We hear dat
him did have a doctor shop; people say him take her
from him father kitchen an dem married, but
de family never like it so they turn dem out.

"Everything was going on all right, but him
tek in sick and dead leaving her with nothing
but de yard; three children to school and feed,
and her heart was full. Mass Albert start to help out.
We know something was going on when him donkey
start to bray early in de morning at her window,
and truth be told, Mass Albert stay there
long after sun gone down".

The women knew when something welled
although she stayed inside, keeping the Kitchen Bitch
down low, sipping bitter cerasee tea, month after month.

It was a boy, and ever since, they said,
she raged at nothing else: the washbelly son
she loved and loathed –
our Uncle Rick, her passion child, her sin.

Not knowing what to make of whispers,
but sure that shame should line our eyes,
we clambered on our uncle's back, counting days
of sun we'd need to get our skin like his – rippling oily
chocolate. We laid our cheeks against

the valleys on his back, his wince reminding us
of tambrin switches for the wasted water,
chickens trampled; speckled puppies lost;
for running round half-naked in the sun,
spoiling our *good* skin.

We never saw our uncle shed a tear,
but like the stubborn nut-grass that overtook
the Joseph Coat outside Miss Brown's sash window
with no glass, a muted turmoil settled in his eyes.

We stuffed mintballs and ginger in our grips,
climbed on Mr. Excel's bus and rumbled back to Kingston,
leaving this beginning in the shadow of the valley
at Above Rocks, until another decade passed
and in the dead of night, carrying her cardboard
boxes stuffed with oats and bible,
Grannie Gillies turned up at the Kencot gate
and the susurrus of women was no more.

IDLEWILD IN AUGUST

Far from the city rattle,
in my retreat behind the country piano,
its keys at rest from the gingery fingers
of a grandfather who loved and ruled

with few breaks in his silence, I stumbled
on a haven that was mine alone – spread out
across old pages that splintered
as I turned them to unearth another time:

adventures that entranced, words that smelled
of sky and sea; of consolation brewed
in Limacol and Lipton's tea,
of love outgrowing loss as Gramma
brushed my hair steeped in rosemary bush
we uprooted from the pearl-pebbles
strung out along our backyard beach.

Idlewild erupted every August
when Kingston schoolyards rested
from their noisy rows of prisoners in their blue
and white, with their inky fingers scrawling over
British kings and queens, parliaments and wars
that tossed their disconnected islands out to sea.

Along the razor rocks and seagrape bush
huddled round the water's yawning edge,
we scampered after cowrie shells
and soldier crabs between our mugs of tambrin tea,
sweet corn and condense milk.

Now, children of the salt and sand, beguiled
by freedom in the wild, we arched our backs
against the wind and vanished in the eddies

of McCarthy's pool, defying sea-egg and mermaid,
till one by one our heads bobbed up anew,
like calabashes floating in the unbroken blue
stretched out along the spine of Idlewild.

Seasoned to the bone,
our sinews contoured on the edge-cliffs
of the creek, we threw off British history,
simmered in our praisesongs, gospels ringing
in our ears, laying tracks of who we were,
of what we would become!

THE STORY OF ROSA AND BASIL

Mama got the visa for America!
Grannie Gillies came to take the front room
and vowed to bring us from the brink of badness
where, she said, Kingston planted us.

As a weekly warning, she wove the spell
of winding roads that snatched her own-way Rosa
from the healing streams of Hector's River;
of that damn country boy who strutted up from Idlewild
with Brylcream hair and his brother's two-toned shoes;
of how these two force-ripe children, green as guinea grass,
swapped school books for trouble.

Her eyes flashed red, her lips trembled
as she paused so we could "jus' imagine them
on that wicked tramcar, skylarking through the street!"
– her lovely light-skin daughter, image of her father,
who sacrificed so much, wrapped himself in the belly
of a banana boat till he uncoiled himself
to make something of chilling life in England –
their Rosa, starched and stamped for Holy Childhood –
until that Basil set her skin on fire.

"It would be Rosa," Grannie Gillies wailed, "she was
always hard-ears." Her face came down to ours,
making sure we pictured them – our mother and our father –
burning up across the tramcar aisle.

Here, she would pause, folded in a shroud of silence,
catching her breath and ours, gathering her strength,
her finger straightening in our faces,
eyes dark as she unfurled the drama:
how they abandoned Sunday School and bible,
and found themselves in bad company at the seaside;

how they washed away the mutterings of old women;
threw away their future over poppy-show,
caught up in the elation of their wanting –
though what they wanted, they never knew;

and Grannie Gillies never said.

THE END OF THAT STORY

She always stopped the story at that place.
The rest we lived with them in the afterlight,
where the morning heat wilted the untried Rosa
and seared her Basil's face, through broken windows
at the sides of houses with no veranda shade.

Their shoulders drooping underneath the weight
of hurried infants, they raged at each other,
forgetting what they had before the eagle swooped,
and tore their papery dreams to shreds.

The rest we saw ourselves: their search
for photographs of picket fences lined
with bougainvillea; their faces drained
from shifty promises and regret drawn out,
swallowing whatever chose to lodge inside their throats;

my mother's hands pressed across our mouths
smothering our protests from the harbour-sharks
next door, waiting for another tale to garnish
at their gate and shame us when we passed;

how my father's gaze fixed itself between
the blades of uncut grass, shutting out the sight
of our patent-leather shoes receding

in the mist of separation; how he gloved
himself in silence, and shunned the mourning dove
that settled in our place, fingering the texture

of our parting – box after box with nothing
more to give: one child sent to the valley
of Above Rocks, one to shady corridors in town,

the third to the womb of Idlewild
to live among dried flowers pressed into
the pages of a world of Whispering Hope.

And I knew then,
as now, the treachery of the ocean and the moon —
how they slip you in the glare of truthful day
that strips away the bark of brittle love!

A GIRL AND A WOMAN

Blue and yellow ribbons streaming through your braids,
you leap sure-footed in between the shadows
dappled in the hopscotch squares she chalked into the pavement.
Dancing in between the fallen petals,
you leave your mother's musings at your back,
disowning all the sorrow that creeps
into her eyes when you're not looking.

Child of sunrise,
let go your mother's trembling,
the snarling weeds that choked her yesterdays,
her memories that fade to black too soon.
Her fingers curling round your hand,
this woman shows you to a road
that she has known too well
but you don't have to take it.

Call her stories lies;
vanish at the crossing,
trail the golden butterfly that you alone can see.

Leave her to her sighs,
to the dampened rosebuds
you crushed between your fingers
and pressed into her hand.
Dart into the mist
of your becoming –
eternity firing your eyes.

PART TWO

ONLY WHEN I WRITE

BOYS

At ten we hated them, their flatness
and their roughness, their sweaty hands
groping in the dirt for marbles;
shouting for us to play their nasty games.
They never wanted books, dolls, secrets
we girls giggled at. They were so loud.

At twelve we whispered names of one or two,
different from the rest. Fifteen –
I looked into his eyes, my nose just inches
from his face. He said it was his father's aftershave.

LESSONS FOR YOUNG WOMEN

Proper English words were not enough
to teach the serious lessons girls must learn.

Only stories of who fell, or proverbs in Jamaica talk
could do the job. From morning until night

doomsday sayings echoed, breaking silences
that drizzled in between: what it meant to be a big girl,

knowing only one woman can live inside the house
so since is not you paying rent, it can't be you.

If you flying past yuh nest, tek sleep mark death
and call back; otherwise you soon find out

what happen to dem force-ripe girls
who paint them lip and ass in red

and hang up hang up at the gate, with all dem
old bwoy bwoy from down the road. Show me yuh company

an ah tell you who you are, for crab who walk too much
always los' him claw and if you sleep wid dawg,

you must get up wid flea. For what sweet nanny goat,
always run dem belly and what gone bad a morning

can't come good a evening! So if you think you bad,
an you ears don't have no hole, gwan you ways

but mine you don't cut off you nose, an spite you face!

YOUNG LOVE

At sixteen, my big sister was a princess
floating on a wind, covered in organdie frills
my mother gathered every night for weeks
and stitched onto the satin sheath
that wrapped her girlishness into a glove.

At midnight sharp, the music stopped.
The stilled house emptied into Sunday.
A wall of rain shut out the street,
pressed the mud against our gate, burying hibiscus.

On the other side,
beyond my comprehension,
that boy Charles sat all day on his veranda,
waiting for the rain to lift
so he could get a glimpse of her,
who, shivering with cold, peering through
the mist to find his eyes, muttered to me,
"Shut up! I said he's not my boyfriend!"

AWAKENING

The moon's white ribbon draped the sandy shore
at our feet. "Only You" (The Platters)
floated on the wind that blew
a briny drizzle through my hair. Your breath warmed
my face; your hands meandered, skin on skin,
uncertain how the fire started by itself. Your body
above mine, shutting out the world.

I knew, not knowing how I knew, that it was time.
On one beat, the waves came in,
the music faded, lights went out.
A flame fluttered, billowed, soared:
stillness in motion, silence in sound.

You breathed, I breathed.

The sand was cold beneath my back.
To the wafting mist of Craven A, a salty droplet slid
along my cheek: for everything, for nothing;
for the flawless rings of smoke
you blew into my eyes; out into the stillness
to await another time when the shadow
of your absence would come to shadow mine.

BLUE NIGHTS, GREY DAYS AT MONA

Wedges of black sky between the moon
and the window of my first-year room,
darkened doors I longed to open,
muffling the urgent hearts of a hundred girls,
circling forbidden fruit of life away from home.

This was the furnace from which 'Sir'
had come, with his *Bachelor of Arts*
and his stories of our sister islands,
igniting our dimly-lit classroom, breaking
through our seventeen-year-old haze,
with his flaring words and curled lips,
razing plans to master Olivetti, and swap
our jippy-jappa hats for filmy stockings,
stiletto heels and narrow skirts tailored
for our destinies on Harbour Street.

This was what he'd said, awaited those
bold enough to sneer at such small dreams –
this hall of tunnels with its endless night,
half-finished women drowning in black ink,
bleary-eyed from Hamlet's conundrums,
middle passages and Gray's Anatomy!
This would be the time, he'd said,
when our trembling buds would burst and flower.

Now, here we were – wide-eyed virgins blinded
in the glare of too much light, skinless
in this godless Eden, cringing in the flame
of too much knowing: hieroglyphics, ifs and shoulds
that swallowed up our souls and gave us back
hydra-headed questions; never answers!

Weighed down with the albatross of freedom,

we held our breath at every intersection
in this town with wrong turns everywhere.
Lonely to the bone, I shrank from flaming coals
of longing, from icy isolation. My feet grew
wooden in the quicksand; they ached for old
sure-footed Sunday steps to Holy Cross.
I longed for the hum of my mother's machine,
for lessons strewn among her common pins,
for pieces of myself I had misplaced;
for sleep unbroken by impatient morning
calling me too soon to choose:
that arrow I craved, to speed me to experience,
that bow, to stay me in my innocence.

SEDUCTION

Across the crowded room I watched your eyes
persuading flowing skirts that they should rise,
convincing women what a blessing you would be.
I saw how charmed you were by your own voice
how hard for you to make another choice,
endangering your ears with words
of those without the wit and elegance of yours.
I sipped my wine and glared, seething
as you stalked us all and walked away.
All through the night I fought you, revolted
as the others fell, loathing the game
you played and everything about you.

And now I hate the morning light
shining on my body next to yours.

AFTER THE HURT

A still and deepening hunger ushers in
the hour that falls behind the paling moon.
In this dark room we share part of ourselves
measuring the meeting of our eyes,
cautioning each other with reminders
of a darkness we have known too well.
To the left is a door we shall not open;
behind it drips the bleeding of old pain.
We glance across the space between our fear –
                bookends with no books.

A ROOM MATE'S SILENCE

At nights, a manic bird beat the air outside
our window, until its final shriek lanced
the fleshy sky and fell among the tatters
of a red Christmas balloon.

The Lenten rituals passed us by although
the priest in purple vestments
whispered at our stations of the cross
and *miserere* floated in the incense
that filled the hostile streets.
In our room, a candle drowned in its own river
and our Holy Saturday vigil was in darkness.

The bottle slipped from her slackening fingers,
emptying bright oval pills all round her bed.
I watched her through the night, seesawing
from the opiate of a shining stillness
to the throbbing world that called and called
her back, but got no answer.

Sometimes choking on dry sand,
sometimes swallowing glass, I slept
the broken sleep of bedlam's child
and, in between, filled thirteen pages –
spitting out the stones and knots
I knew had churned inside her
and could fill me instead.

The sun rose on an ordinary morning.
I threw the window open, still fingering the edges
of the deep, dark hole of trembling days.
I stared into the nuances of a sky that stunned,
I breathed the new air breaking through the mist.

The horses flashed their tails into the morning's face,
cantering through the fields outside our door.
The scattered banyan leaves whirring
in the wind, echoed the rustling tails of humming birds,
and bees busy at their honey pots across Chapel Gardens.

I threw myself onto the poui carpet,
petals fallen from those trees already sporting
broad-rimmed hats of new blooms bursting into light.

Steel pan hallelujahs soared into the morning,

                                       into her silence.

ONE OF US IS MISSING

We loved you only yesterday when we were young;
when stars stopped by to hear you sing.

We loved you only yesterday
When moonlit stairways led to magic kingdoms
and golden poui petals cushioned every fall.
We loved you only yesterday when we whispered
all our dreams into the Mona sky.

Our laughter faded,
our glory years lay drying
in the shadows of the disappearing day.

The stars stopped by last night to hear you sing
but found you locked in silence.
At dusk a hand fell on your shoulder,
taking you – your fingers
groping in the darkness for a light.

You never knew the bow was bent
– the arrow drawn and stiff –
until you heard the songbird in the evening
and smiled into the night.

ONLY WHEN I WRITE

(Psychiatrist: So do you rage and scream your anger and disappointment or
show your joy so others know what's going on with you?
Patient: Only when I write)

She swallows hard stony phrases
knotting in her throat at someone's cruel barbs.
Bracing her shoulders, she tilts her head away,
stifling her protest behind a thinning smile.
None of it is worth the fight.

She turns to watch a yellow bird, a stream of water
whispering on the hillside. She turns to share
the moment, forgetting no-one's there.
Melodies she might have sung,
words she could have blasted out
keep buzzing in her head, prickling in her hair.

At night a grey rectangle lies waiting
as she keys in the day's business.
Her fingers on the keyboard release images
that float from where she buried them all day.
The screen filled, she quickens at the sight
of what stares back, quaking at this storm
of words, this bane, this balm, this other self that's free
and freeing, although it startles her with truths
she doesn't want to stare her in the face.

COMING HOME

Awakened by the glare
of cabin lights switched on
before our landing, I throw
the blanket from my feet, unravelling myself
from hopes that thrive on distance.

How forget all I knew
passing across your mountain mantle,
your brokenness and drought?
How forget your naked children
slipping on the smears of death
on bullet-ridden floors?
As if your bougainvillea blooms
had not seduced me before
to forget their thorns.

The wings arc down,
flirting with the ocean's open face,
shadowing the blazing sand.
Insistent rhythms stir in half-forgotten places
where I hid my painting book of children laughing.
My carefree minute stretches till the sudden thud
of wheels upon the steaming tarmac;
the engine's shrieks that tell me I am home.

Stirring from their perch along
the prison-wire circling the island,
all three of Marley's little birds still wail:
"Don't worry 'bout a thing,
every little thing will be all right."

Their meagre truth wears thin.

OCTOBER MORNINGS

Among October's turning leaves
A thousand butterflies erupt
onto the sidewalk sporting shades
of yellow along their wings,
mirroring the children's sunny ribbons.

Near to the church, sudden shots ring out;
their laughter interrupted, the children scatter
from the shattered glass, choking on the exhaust
from the Nissan speeding with its dead.
The butterflies' wings lie wilted in cold blood.

After the rain, the mountains rest awash
against the sky, like pencilled v's and w's scrawled
across a child's uncertain page.
Poinsettias stretch their necks and arms in waiting;
the sun winks at the valley, promising to shine.

But the dark days were too long;
the blood on the land too thick,
the flood of our grief too strong,
so the rivers crashed their banks
washing the land out to sea;
the tree-tops had no blossoms,
and the peel-head john crow circles
watching us dance with death.

THE CRACK

Stay away, regret, nobody wants you now;
I knew you would be lurking here tonight,
waiting to fall around me
like twisted stockings round the shrivelled skin
of an old woman journeying too long.

Back off, regret, you won't break in this time –
I hid away the carols and the baubles;
I turned my back on pine-shaped trees
whose smell brings you too close against
my door. When children's voices filled the air
with promises of peace and joy,
I pulled my shutters down.
So what's that knocking at my ribs?
A whirring fan with dusty circles of stale air
just spins and spins. "The Little Drummer Boy"
tiptoes in through a crack under my door
and in the instant that I pause to notice,
Regret, you walk right in.

HOLY SATURDAY

On Saturday evening, alleluia
soars with domino and dancehall
across a yard of zinc that thrums, deflecting
string and bass against my stomach wall.

As rising incense blurs the smell of weed
the worn-out priest snorts to clear his head
pleading for a hearing. He strains across
the yawning congregation distracted by
loose backyard images: body parts sway
until they fume and fall into the foreplay
that leads to love or death.

And when we walk the Easter Bible story,
and the reader comes to Peter's three denials,
the rooster next door obliges.
Silence holds for a second
and then the cacophony rises:
sound system and organ in one!

THE SEARCH

How strange that we should sip at once
both peace and poison from this cup
raised by priests and sorcerers,
chanting alleluias amid the incense-bearing altar boys,
insensate hordes of pilgrims lost,
groping in the teeming murk for light,
finding only this eternity of night.

How strange to search,
to finger baubles,
not knowing there's a difference
between the thinly layered gloss we crave
and hammered gold that outlasts the grave.

BIRTHDAY PARTY

So now the numbers shout
and everyone is counting the meaning of your life,
adding up your stocks and bonds,
numbering the real estate. Two-thirds
of all you'll ever be is gone
and what is left feels like it's losing ground
though, perhaps, your net worth isn't down.

But when you do the reckoning yourself,
it's other things that count: a one-inch scar
across your knee; a rocking chair at Idlewild;
the burnt-out mound of everything you had;
the boy behind the column, his eyes ablaze
when suddenly he saw what Hamlet felt inside;
the crumpled note your daughter pressed
into your hand, her day too filled for words.

You shudder still and shed warm tears at lovers
in the moonlight. The hairs along your arm still rise
when you relive him reading you *Gibran*,
his perfect smoke-rings misting in your eyes.
So now, you watch them raise
thin vessels in your praise, while you lament the hollow
down inside and swallow hard for something light to say,
yearning for one true thing –
one thing that will endure beyond the day.

LONELY IS...

... a river where the ripples have no stones,
a shadow lengthening down a slender room,
a lullaby without an infant's eyes
fluttering to sleep; lonely is
the stillness of a loveless April evening;
a night of silence broken
by a fan that makes no difference;
a leaf entangled in a spider's web,
a thread unravelled from its weave.

Lonely is a woman on day seven of her waiting,
picking up to check for dial tone, then sinking
to a floor with just her footsteps to be wiped.
Lonely is a locket lying open with no portrait;
a broken music box without its song.

Lonely is the memory of a time long gone,
a moment when you pause and hear your breath
without another breath to comfort you.
Mankind in his loneliness is made to turn to God
But lonely is a God who turns away
distanced by the image of himself in His creation.

JUST FOR NOW

Love, I have known you
in the improbable gentle eyes of a boy
who revved his bike along the summer shore
spraying me with sand, not knowing I was there.
I've felt you in the tremor of my untried lips,
pressed against his urgent mouth. Later
in September, the leaves turning brown,
the sliver of an early moon paused like a comma
in the sky, our hairs on end,
he uncovered me against the twilight wind
and your fingers closed round my trembling heart.

Love, I've heard you in forbidden whispers
shared with someone else on borrowed time.
I've tasted your bitter and your sweet,
watching too many backs recede.
You've left me on fire, simmering in your glow,
whimpering in the embers when someone had to go.
I've searched for you among the early blossoms,
remembering to shield myself from thorns.
And yes… I've turned from you, weary
of the dried petals that always followed you.

I've eluded you and longed for you,
but now we meet again
I know I mustn't count the beads of sorrow
nor ask about tomorrow;
I must embrace you Love, if only just for now.

MAMMOGRAM

The cotton cloth falls softly round her shoulders,
its pale blue stars and light pinstripes
gazing upon coloured dots and dashes –
a wishing-well at rest upon her back.

In a hollow room, the width of three school rulers,
(six the length), a sickening yellow paint crawls
up the walls, glancing at a bulbless socket.
A dull, rusting hook receives her blouse.

Her cold skin growing wrinkles,
the metal monster waits, invented by
some man who's never known
the tenderness of a woman's breast.

With the right to see what she can't see
inside her, it irons out her flesh,
grumbling to a stop, clamping round her breast,
snapping shut, spitting out hieroglyphics

to be deciphered by this boy
she never saw until he pulled that door
between her hoping and her certainty,
clasping his proud clipboard.

The metal god has found the fickle phantom
burrowing soundlessly inside,
gnawing at sacs that nestled her infants;
boring through the cherished mound where
his love found rest…

drawing out her life.

DADDA'S PROMISE

When yesterdays outnumbered their tomorrows
and time's uncaring march denied old sorrows,

when his footsteps slowed beside the mossy stones
and listless evening stretched out in his bones,

his whisper lingered when darkness thinned:
"I'll come inside the morning wind

and wrest the salt from drowsing seagrape leaves.
My fingers will find yours among the sheaves

of straw, and as you turn old lullabies,
my lips will kiss that longing from your eyes.

When you breathe the brackish air that rises
from the sea at Idlewild, I'll be there.

The almond leaves will sweep the wind across your face
retracing journeys time cannot erase.

When your dreams recoil from unwelcome night
I'll take your hand; we'll hurry to the light."

GRAMMA'S LOSS

Dadda's Friday shirts were cambric blue,
starched and ironed to a sheen,
his tie a darker shade of cotton
knotted at his throat, his hat – Tyrolean straw –

she'd trimmed herself with strips of red on grey.
Day in day out he rode the fix-wheel Raleigh
to Llanrumney, his trouser cuffs folded back
with bicycle clips she bought from Haber's haberdashery,

to keep him safe from whirring chains strung
between the spokes that spun below the rack
where she clipped the shut-pans down
– white enamel with blue lips –

always warm with home-brewed soup and solace,
sipped among banana leaves, far from
the wagging tongues of reapers
with their machetes glinting in the sun,

sneaking a look at "backra-massa spy,
wid him three eye dat neva shut",
who swallowed resentment when Dadda counted up
the bunches, chopped and boxed between the beads

of steaming sweat, by fingers shaded in banana stain,
trailing drops of blood to Oracabessa port –
the same hate Dadda felt when face to face
with shifting eyes of sallow colonizers.

When he came home to Idlewild, bearing the weight
of brownness tethered in his brows,
she gentled him with stories of his children
and their children at the seaside;

of their coconut bats and breadfruit balls,
wickets made of seaweed, a pitch marked out
along the craggy sand behind the house,
where his sons mimicked plantation,

and nieces giggled at the strangeness of a game
without an end. She told him how they scrambled
after soldier-crabs that spilled from stony crevasses;
of how one latched himself on Patsy's lips

and sent her into Gramma's arms for hushing
and cream biscuit smeared with marmalade.
And though he set his jaw in that straight line
of silence in her bed, she never questioned once

the tremor in his breast for her, for every child they lost
or bore, for babies sent from Kingston for the right beginning.
On that last day he wore his cambric blue;
Gramma made the cross herself – with coffee roses

culled outside their window. She closed the door
upon his Olivetti and took to counting hours
on the wicker chair, loosening her hair as if in waiting
for when his fingers would come running through.

PORT MARIA PARISH CHURCH

The battle was brief and to the point,
with no punctuation – just like the sentences
my father whispered, his voice and eyes
owning knotty rumours curdling in his bones.

Knowing Death was eyeing him he asked to make
his way once more along Galina's skirting board
past the Lighthouse Road and Wilderness to Idlewild,
but something hurrying at his back

passed him at the turn and tripped him
to the ground. So we made the crossing for him –
a convoy round familiar turns that brought him
to the edge where nothing moved

but almond leaves muttering in December
breeze, under the brow of firefly where
Gramma's plaited mats had lain,
while we whispered village stories at a

distance safe enough from Noel Coward's
hilltop resting place. The sun streamed through
the windows stained with sea and sand.
We laid him within Dadda's reach, inches from the brother

no-one understood. Now enfolded in damp earth,
facing the unnamed island planted in the blue
across from Padgee Beach, my father's silence found no foe.
Soon Gramma laid her head among her men

– her two sons and a husband –
where each could hear the other's call
and bring home anyone who lost the way,
to watch the sea gulls hover in the bay

and hear the morning murmur in the
foaming sand, mantled by the grey
and indigo, under the seraph's wings
stretched out across the way to Idlewild.

MY GRAMMA CLEO

At dawn she smelled of Idlewild,
of sea-salt air, steaming morning mint,
La India hair oil and Limacol spilled
on a four-poster home of young dreams.

I knew her in warm, secret places –
a nook in the curve of her arm,
old houses that doubled as church,
where pain was eased with blue teacups
and home was her brushed-away hurt.

I watched her chase flickering fireflies
as night breeze played in her hair,
and love was the depth in her eyes.
Some nights she smelled of dry pages,
of faraway places yellowed with age,
of Sunday school songs his spent fingers urged
from a piano listlessly dying.

Lately she lives in a place beyond loss,
where barren walls echo her footfalls;
she crosses old paths with a stranger's feet
and longs for the balm of dusk lilies.

...AND GENTLY GO...

Some say the sun still rises at the break
of day; that sparrows hover still, their fluttering

wings stirring the leaves just like this ache
that stirs inside me when I wake to see the trembling

of your eyelids and I find instead this space
that's lived beside me since your breath vanished

in the evening mist, leaving your face
so cold against my touch. Oh how I wished

I could have warmed you. Where must I walk
without your hand in mine? Emptiness ensnares

me and I stumble. Inside, the ticking clock
reminds me of the nightfall and my fears

of moonlight without you. My footsteps slow.
The shadows dance across the wall, old curtains part.

I take your outstretched hand and gently go
into the light enfolding you, stilling my heart.

THE PIANO

The naseberry bleeds white when cut too soon
and coffee roses wither when the moon
is down. Their songs receded to the hill
but even now the piano haunts me still.

It takes me to the scented space between
embroidered sheets. It brings me every flicker
of that flame that used to throw a softening glow
inside the Home Sweet Home, as shiny pennies

slipped between my fingers, skidding
on the floorboards of our makeshift Sunday school.
It lingers in the choruses of all things bright
and beautiful, all creatures great and small,

recalling the echoes in the half-lit passages
between two chilly rooms where images
of dying loomed and souls turned inside
out while lovers wept into the tide.

ONE MAN AND HIS DOG

April – my fiftieth year – a Sunday stolen
from our helter-skelter lives in scattered cities,
we stretch out in the sunstreams –
four sisters counting rhinestones in the sand.

From the corners of our eyes we sense
each other's musings, take slanted glances
at our mother, purse our lips, and swallow deep –
concede the unnamed detail lurking just behind her eyes.

A fisherman leaves his prints along the beach,
his dreadlocks glistening from his daybreak swim
across the bay, his tackle and his dog in tow.
A smile eludes the mask our mother wears these days;

the corners of her mouth slowly upturned,
she stuns us with a bygone song "One man
and his dog went to mow the meadow",
pointing at the Dread, her eyes fixed ahead.

Just then, her face dissolves into a face
owned by another time and place:
1962 – the year of Independence,
when she'd bundled up her pardner draw

with all the other savings to pay down
on her key. How her eyes had shone,
fingering her machine with its motor
quickening her stitches, turning corners,

embroidering the patterns of tomorrow
on curtains for a house that was a home.
Now we watch her turn to face the breakers
rippling into shore, salty water brimming everywhere.

ASH WEDNESDAY, 2002

Beyond the greyness of a grey-blue sky,
the whispering wind daunted by your laughter
lurching to a choking fear;
beyond the halting of an aimless day,
the plummet to the sea you never trusted
– no ground beneath your feet –
your eyes startled – a fleeting thought of elsewhere;
beyond the shirt they parted searching for
a hint of life eliding…

beyond the gaping hole inside our daughter's heart
– a child with half herself,

                                nowhere to be found;
beyond a leafless tree, a song cut short,
dry petals strewn across a walkway
sprinkled with our tears; beyond a sigh into
a swirling tempest:
                   nothing more?

MY DAUGHTER GROWS UP

Silence stretches out on
a dusty window sill
where a father's laughter lived;
where trappings of his living linger still,

until she culls them gently one
by one into a swollen bag,
leaving spaces clean between
the dust. Her shoulders sag

with tired disbelief.
She leans against the door
emptying his smell
in bottles on the floor
littered with the clearing
of what used to be assurance.
A salty bubble welling,
she turns to meet my glance.

Her eyes are older now;
Her face no longer wears
unsullied hope. The woman
in her steadies. She bears
her loss with grace, doing
what she must; fingering
a smudgy photograph,

another time, enduring.

THE DREAM

Through the veil that hung
between our worlds, I saw
your face astonished as you watched
her broken in the night, aching for the morning
to undo the treachery of the sea
that swallowed you, enclosing bright blue
afternoon inside that deep, dark stillness.

Then came a sudden light
belonging somewhere else,
not earth. It beamed across your face
smoothing out the worry on your brow
settling you at last, in that silent place
with no more pain, where you will be her angel.

REUNION 2003

The last visitor is gone.
Backed against the spaces of a yawning room,
I watch the raindrops smear the window pane
where yesterday their shadows danced.
Silence sweats along the sill
rising with the curtain's frill
as it brushes random relics of three faces
that only yesterday broke into laughter
at nothing more than being there: Mama's *Daily Word*
lies open on the last page of the visit;
a toothbrush bearing Donna's fingerprints;
nearby the unanswered question of her candy-cane
left to an army of unyielding ants,
distracted from a ball of orphaned socks.

I strip the sheets with their enduring smells:
oil of wintergreen from Marjorie's hands
spreading ease across our mother's back;
a pillow stained with splashes of bay rum;
the ash from coils we burned to silence mosquitoes.
Strands of plaited straw unravelling everywhere,
my island shrinks, suspended in the cadence
of another emptying.

P.S. — 2006

Last May, we scorned the new highway
and sought our family of winding roads
from Kingston through the Junction back to Idlewild.
Still framed in blue, still locked in by the cove

of consolation, the spot behind the almond tree bears
a rough-hewn frame and uprights longing for the day
they will become a house. Unfinished columns
raise their rusting steel into the sky.

The upstairs house across the street,
where I gulped Miss Connell's kerosene oil and gave
Gramma conniptions, is closer to its falling.
The graves, no longer painted, hold their ground

along the road before the bend deepens to Galina;
we glance, not fearing ghosts. We know that when
the first world corners this strip of island,
even they will disappear like our soldier crabs —

not borrowed from their shells by childish pranks —
but gone for good, as if they'd never been.
His shack planted where our cut-stone wall
had stood against thunder and lightning,

the coconut vendor wonders at the wonder
in our eyes, oblivious to the meanings swirling
in that sea we owned, against that sky
that sheltered who we were.

And up the street, that other land lies bare,
the hibiscus hedge that made it ours, gone;
instead the unkempt trees, the flowers and the garbage —
ramshackle spread from Kingston to Galina.

The water tank stands still and dry, its children
and grandchildren scattered in the lands of frost,
still longing for their sun that knows no season. No one
to claim this place that knows the shape of every hurt,

of every dent in hearts that found their way
from intersected lives to breathe its balm;
no sign of Gramma's altar cloths and patchwork spreads;
no plaited straw,
                    no lullaby,
                              no brown girl in de ring.

THE BOATMAN

The boat comes in slowly.
Like oversized linen handkerchiefs
its sails grow stiff against the sky.
The bowsprit rises in the twilight mist,
falls in the ocean spray. On the shore,

the old woman waits, her face framed in a held breath.
Sighting the boatman, she basks in the smile
she knows. Her eyes lock with his, assured
he's coming for her, certain he'll calm
that rattling inside her threadbare soul.

Long hidden, with thoughts she had misplaced,
the child inside her stirs, flailing her arms
through the salt-thick air, her toes hooked
in oozing sand, the sunburnt hairs raised on her skin
dancing in the wind. Her child-heart pounds
breaking through her chest
like the pulse of a startled bird. Eyes fixed,
mouth agape, she sees now his facelessness –
a grotesque mask askew where calming eyes had been,
and for the smile she'd seen before, a chilling smirk.

The boat comes to a halt.
Companions of the boatman huddle
in a shining light that stills the flutter
in the woman's breast, settling the child in her.
His face is gentle now; he takes her outstretched hand,
easing her aboard into the swathing glow.

Now emptied of the terror and the child, she steps across
the bridge between unsure and certain,
through the light between the mist and meandering waves
under the veil of lighted gossamer.

The waves stretch out across the sand,
their fingers reaching for the cool of evening.

NEW POETRY FROM PEEPAL TREE PRESS
Spring-Summer 2009

Marion Bethel
Bougainvillea Ringplay
ISBN: 9781845230845; pp. 88, July 2009; £7.99

These poems are sensual in the most literal sense – the poems are about the senses, the smell of vanilla and sex, the sound of waves – radio, voices, sea; the taste of crab soup; the texture of hurricane wind, and the chaos of colours bombarding the eye. Bahamian poetry is being defined in the work of Marion Bethel.

Jacqueline Bishop
Snapshots from Istanbul
ISBN: 9781845231149; pp. 80, April 2009; £7.99

Framed by poems that explore the lives of the exiled Roman poet Ovid, and the journeying painter Gaugin, Bishop locates her own explorations of where home might be. This is tested in a sequence of sensuous poems about a doomed relationship in Istanbul, touching in its honesty and, though vivid in its portrayal of otherness, highly aware that the poems' true subject is the uprooted self.

Mahadai Das
A Leaf in His Ear
ISBN: 978900715591; pp. 160, May 2009; £9.99

The selection includes the whole of *Bones* and *My Finer Steel Will Grow*, and most of the poems from her first collection, *I Want to Be a Poetess of My People*, as well as many of the fine poems published in journals and previously uncollected – from lively, humorous nation-language poems to the oblique, highly original poems written in the years after *Bones*.

Kwame Dawes
Hope's Hospice
with images by Joshua Cogan
ISBN: 9781845230784; pp. 72, April 2009; £7.99

Powerfully illustrated by Joshua Cogan's photographs, Kwame
Dawes's poems make it impossible to see HIV/AIDS as something
that only happens to other people. Here, AIDS becomes the channel
for dramas that are both universal and unique, voices that are
archetypal and highly individual – dramas of despair and stoicism,
deception and self-honesty, misery and joy in life.

Millicent A.A. Graham
The Damp in Things
ISBN: 9781845230838; pp. 56, May 2009; £7.99

In *The Damp in Things*, we are invited into the unique imagination of
Millicent Graham: she offers us a way to see her distinctly contem-
porary and urban Jamaica through the slant eye of a surrealist, one
willing to see the absurdities and contradictions inherent in its
society. These are poems about family, love, spirituality, fear, and
above all desire, where the dampness of things is as much about the
humid sensuality of this woman's island as it is about her constant
belief in fecundity, fertility and the unruliness of the imagination.

Esther Phillips
The Stone Gatherer
ISBN: 9781845230852; pp. 72, May 2009; £7.99

Tracing a woman-centred movement from childhood to the contem-
plative maturity of elder and prophet, Esther Phillips's affecting new
collection is the work of a poet of wit, intelligence, and maturity of
vision. She uses poetry to test the meaning of experience, and to seek
and find its grace notes. Located in the moving, breathing landscape
of Barbados, and displaying a lyrical West Indian English, this
collection marks her as a major poetic voice.

Jennifer Rahim
Approaching Sabbaths
ISBN: 9781845231156; pp. 129, July 2009; £8.99

There is a near perfect balance between the disciplined craft of the poems, and their capacity to deal with the most traumatic of experiences in a cool, reflective way. Equally, she has the capacity to make of the ordinary something special and memorable. The threat and reality of fragmentation – of psyches, of lives, of a nation – is ever present, but the shape and order of the poems provide a saving frame of wholeness.

Tanya Shirley
She Who Sleeps with Bones
ISBN: 9781845230876; pp. 76, April 2009; £7.99

'In the deftly searching poems of *She Who Sleeps With Bones*, Tanya Shirley considers how memory revolts from oblivion, what it can mean to be "haunted by the fruit" of desire – sexual, political, the desire for an "uncomplicated legacy," for home when home exists only as a memory we cannot trust entirely, a space we fear even as we continue to go back there. These poems startle, stir, provoke equally with their intelligence and their music. A wonderful debut.'
— Elizabeth Nunez, author of *Prospero's Daughter*

All Peepal Tree titles are available from the website
www.peepaltreepress.com
with a money back guarantee, secure credit card ordering and fast delivery throughout the world at cost or less.

Peepal Tree Press is celebrated as the home of challenging and inspiring literature from the Caribbean and Black Britain. Subscribe to our mailing list for news of new books and events. Contact us at:
Peepal Tree Press, 17 King's Avenue, Leeds LS6 1QS, UK
Tel: +44 (0) 113 2451703 E-mail: contact@peepaltreepress.com